PHAETHON

Euripides

PHAETHON

Reconstructed from the fragments
and translated
by ALISTAIR ELLIOT

OBERON BOOKS
LONDON

This version of *Phaethon* first published in 2008 by Oberon Books Ltd
Electronic edition published in 2012

Oberon Books Ltd
521 Caledonian Road, London N7 9RH
Tel: 020 7607 3637 / Fax: 020 7607 3629
e-mail: info@oberonbooks.com
www.oberonbooks.com

A catalogue record for this book is available from the British Library.

PB ISBN: 978-1-84002-897-3
E ISBN: 978-1-84943-654-0

eBook conversion by Replika Press PVT Ltd, India.

Visit www.oberonbooks.com to read more about all our books and to
buy them. You will also find features, author interviews and news of
any author events, and you can sign up for e-newsletters so that you're
always first to hear about our new releases.

Contents

Preface

Anyone who has sat in the Theatre of Dionysus on the side of the Acropolis hill and looked out at that wonderful distracting view of the city, the mountains and the gulf, will wonder how Euripides could have converted the myth of Phaethon into a play. Aeschylus had shown an audience here the Caucasus, with Prometheus chained to a rock and a vulture anticipated at any moment; and numerous caves and even islands had been represented on that narrow and not very deep oblong of stage. But this story would seem to demand even more of that small space.

The myth is fairly simple. 'Everyone knows' that the sun crosses the sky in a chariot driven by the sun-god Helios. One day, either the god allowed his quite young son Phaethon to drive the solar chariot, or Phaethon 'stole' – that is, took – the chariot and tried to do the job himself. He wasn't able to control the immortal horses and the chariot went off course (scorching the 'Indians' and the people of Africa so that they ever afterwards had dark skins). Phaethon died in the crash or was killed by a thunderbolt thrown by Zeus (to save the world, not to mention Olympus).

How was the four-horse chariot of the sun, the sun burning away on it, and a catastrophe among the constellations, to be seen in broad daylight? Of course, all that must happen off stage: there can be no scratch of smoke across the sky, no timed lightning or crack of thunder, no splash, no thud. There could be no question of such extraordinary special effects. That sort of thing can be told as part of a story, but not shown on stage, not credibly. But Euripides saw a quite different sort of difficulty in the well-known myth. Somehow a story has the power to make you accept it uncritically, but why would a god let his son try to do something dangerous that he was too young for? This play gives a reasonable explanation: Phaethon was Helios' son all right, but he was not, like an ordinary son, brought up in his father's house, because his mother was married to someone else, King Merops, and Helios had seduced her and made her pregnant. Merops thought Phaethon was his child, and Phaethon thought Merops was his father.

On the fatal day which the play covers, Phaethon's mother Clymene has recently (perhaps in the first scene) told the boy about Helios being his father, and she now also reveals that Helios promised her a favour. If he goes and asks Helios for the favour and Helios grants it, then that will prove her incredible story is true. This explains how Helios was forced (by his promise to Phaethon's mother) to allow the boy to drive the solar chariot. Of course, when Phaethon dies, King Merops wants to know why his boy was allowed to drive the chariot, and the truth comes out, causing a marital row which probably becomes violent and has to be resolved by the interference of a god, possibly Aphrodite, possibly Clymene's father Oceanus.

So far, we can be sure that is a fairly accurate sketch of the plot as Euripides wrote it. Goethe, who attempted a restoration of the play, pointed out that it was not about a cosmic catastrophe (as Ovid describes it in the *Metamorphoses*) but something more intimate: 'We confine ourselves to one narrow contracted locality that might suit the Greek stage.' Our evidence for this plot is the two leaves of a copy of the play which have survived, and a torn piece of papyrus which holds the first sentence or so of a plot-summary – and a few actual lines from the play quoted (usually they are lines without dramatic context) by later writers. However, when the two leaves have been translated (the rest of the text, perhaps eight other leaves, is missing) and the *obviously* missing scenes (the prologue and opening scene, the angry clash between Phaethon and his father, the messenger speech, the marital argument, and the appearance of a god) and some choruses have all been supplied, the play is still too short. At that point complete invention – of structure as well as dialogue – was unavoidable.

It is not easy – in fact, it must be impossible – to keep a reconstruction within the limits of what one knows of fifth-century Athenian thought, but I have tried to write what I thought Euripides might have written. Finally, I have also had always in mind the idea that I should not invent anything that might have stuck in the mind of a reader or member of an audience and been quoted later. Three quarters of Euripides' work survives (if at all) mainly in the form of lines or words that later classical authors have quoted, because they seemed wise or interesting, or included a rare word. I felt I should not compose a single line that might have survived in that way. My aim was always to re-invent the play as seen once in the Theatre of Dionysus in Athens in the spring of some year in the last quarter of the fifth-century BC; I was not trying to make a modern equivalent. I hope that, as a friend put it, it will seem that Euripides 'met me half-way'.

*

I must here acknowledge a deep debt to James Diggle, whose edition of the play was my firm basis, and for his helpful comments and correspondence on some of my solutions to problems of interpretation. He, and my friend Peter Jones, provided a background of scholarly doubt which must have stiffened and improved my work.

Finally, the thought that Jonathan Kent might one day direct the play made me think again about which god might intervene at the end, so that I rewrote the part for Oceanus (the god of water) – which was, I think, more appropriate; and the thought that Roger Hogg might one day act in it has been an inspiration and an encouragement; so that indirectly I owe both of them gratitude too. All errors and anachronisms however are my own.

Alistair Elliot
Newcastle upon Tyne
2007

Characters

CLYMENE, Queen of Ethiopia, daughter of
Oceanus

PHAETHON, her son

HERALD

MEROPS, King of Ethiopia, married to Clymene

TUTOR

NURSE, an old family servant of Clymene's

SERVANT

PEASANT

YOUNG GIRLS, daughters of Merops
and Clymene

OCEANUS, father of Clymene,
god of the encircling sea

*

CHORUS of palace women

PHAETHON

Time: Just before sunrise. Barely light.

Scene: Outside the palace of King MEROPS, in Ethiopia.

*

CLYMENE: Nobody knows my story yet, but now
    I've told my son and he does not believe me.
    I told him: in the year before his birth
    I was seduced – I still feel proud of it –
    By Helios, the golden face of heaven.
    Nobody knew, but Helios and I,
    The pleasure and the fruit. For in that time
    My father gave me to a king in marriage,
    King Merops, and the child seemed born to him,
    The ruler of this country, the first land
    That Helios from his four-horse chariot strikes
    With his golden flame as he goes up the sky.
    Our black-skinned neighbours in this country call it
    Aithiopia – Shining Land or Shining Stables
    Where Dawn and Helios both
    Have shelters for their horses. Hot, of course –
    The god's flame is ferocious going up
    And burns things in the distance, but near home
    He keeps it temperate – marvellously warm.
    We are protected somehow from the danger
    Of the golden ingot though it is so close.

    Daily I come to see it rise – for there
    In his chariot, silent, goes my ancient lover.

PHAETHON comes out of the palace.

What is it, son? Why do you rise so early?

PHAETHON: Good morning, mother. What a night! – all spent
In thinking of the story of my birth.
It troubles me. Why did you have to tell me?
I think I'd rather not have known this truth.
Why have you told me now, and not before?

CLYMENE: Because you're marrying, of course. You have to
know
Your blood and where you come from when you marry.
When a man has a child he looks to see
Familiar features in the little face – and you
Would not see anything of Merops there.
You won't be having children soon, perhaps,
But it seemed to me I had to tell you now –
Before you started. When your bride is here
We may not have another chance to speak.

PHAETHON: I can't help wishing you had never told me.
I seem to be someone different. There's so much
Storming about my mind already. Look –
The marriage that my father has arranged
For me to seal today – to sign with gods –
I am too young for any kind of marriage.
I hardly know myself. I'm standing here
On my last morning as a child. Today
Father is sending me – not out to hunt
Or practise fighting from a chariot –
But to bring back my new contracted wife.
Also, he wants me to be king beside him.

This is so great a change, so much at once.
Mother, I am too young. I am not ready.

CLYMENE: My husband's old. He wishes to secure
The kingdom now while he is wise and well.
It's natural, and you must rise to it.
I understand your feelings – but who is
Ready to be responsible for a kingdom?

PHAETHON: I do not understand the need for marriage.
I have no wish to disobey my father,
But how will being married help me rule?
I really am too young. And father's not so old.

CLYMENE: Merops is not your father. You're the son
Of Helios, worthy of a goddess' bed.

PHAETHON: That's what you say – that's what you keep on saying.
Do mothers always think their sons are gods?

CLYMENE: It ill becomes you, son, to mock the hopes
We have for you: we have no other son,
And we must think, before we leave this world,
Of how to leave you safe: we want you married.

PHAETHON: Can marriage with the daughter of a god
Be safe? I think the mixture would turn sour.

CLYMENE: This is no common mixture: you're as good
As she is. Listen. Listen to me, son:
My father is Oceanus, the god
Of waters who embraces every land
In the round world, and you were born of me:
The seed was not King Merops' – you were planted
In me by the embraces of a god.

PHAETHON: You must have thought about this every day.
    How could you keep so long so great a secret?
    How could you keep my father in the dark?
    I must believe you, but you understand
    I find it hard. How can I know the truth?

CLYMENE: Today you fetch your bride from Helios' palace.
    Before you lift and carry her away,
    The delicate princess, speak to her father:
    Remind him what he promised me, that time
    So long ago, one favour for my beauty.
    It was a solemn promise he must keep.
    Ask what you want – one wish – to ask for more
    Is not allowed – but if you get that wish,
    You are his son; if not, then I'm a liar.

PHAETHON: Well, how do I get near the sun's hot palace?

CLYMENE: He will take care no harm will come to you.

PHAETHON: You're right, he will take care – if he's my father.

CLYMENE: Be sure of that – in due course you will know it.

PHAETHON: Thank you – I don't believe you're telling lies.
    But go indoors, for there I see the maids
    Are coming out, who in my father's palace
    Sweep the rooms every day and keep his treasures
    Shining so bright and make the entrances
    Smell clean and pleasant when they burn some incense,
    Our local frankincense, to air the house.
    And, when my aged father leaves his sleep
    And passes through these doors and speaks to me
    About this marriage, I'll go to Helios' house,
    And test your story, mother, for its truth.

The CHORUS have now come out of the palace. PHAETHON and CLYMENE go in.

CHORUS of palace servant women sing their Entrance Ode. There are three separate tunes here: for stanzas one and two; for stanzas three and four; and the final tune is interrupted (as the words explain) after stanza five, the sixth paragraph being not another stanza but instead a spoken rush of excited dactyls.

CHORUS: Dawn, now, appearing late
    takes her horse across the land,
    while there in flight above my head
    the dancing Pleiades fade away.
    Song in the trees,
    delicate fabrication
    of the nightingale,
    occupies morning with her sobs: Itys –
    Itys her child, her long lament.

    Shepherds walking on the hill
    wake their flutes and move their sheep.
    Young horses, pairs of chestnuts, run
    into the pasture for a feed.
    And hunters now
    eager to make a kill
    go off in line to work,
    while by the waters of Oceanus swans
    are calling sweetly, one to one.

*

    Boats are putting out to sea
    with oars, with useful gusts of wind.
    Up go the sails. The boatmen as they haul
    are chanting, 'Come with us, come Queen of airs,

escort us through the calm when the winds drop,
home to our children and our loving wives' –
the canvas bellies to the forestay rope.

All have work and worries; I
am driven by duty and desire
to sing, to celebrate a wedding day
in form, in song: for when the good days come
for masters, we the servants take heart too,
joy fills our song – but if ill fortune falls,
that weighs upon us all, on the whole house.

*

This daylight of today is marked:
a boundary, the beginning of a marriage
which I have prayed for and have lived to see,
to sing at last the hymeneal song of our dear master:
– The god has given, time has brought about
this wedding for our rulers.
Now let the song of wedding days arise!

But look, it's the king coming out of the palace,
and the holy herald with Phaethon too,
all three together stride out like a team –
We must hold our tongues, choke back our song.
Because he is going to show us his plans
about great matters:
That he wishes to settle his son in the harness
of sacred marriage –
the yoke and bridle of a bride.

MEROPS and PHAETHON have come out of the palace accompanied
by a third person, the HERALD. The HERALD intones rather grandly,
not in ordinary dialogue metre:

HERALD: Inhabitants of the plains beside great Ocean,

Be silent now,

And leave your houses, come outside:

O come and hear

My proclamation of a royal speech:

Pray silence for his words

And fruitfulness for the marriage that he comes

To speak of now,

The father and the son together sealing

A wedding here today: so, silence, all.

MEROPS: It is a moment in a father's life

When he is buffeted by gusts of joy.

But now, if ever, I must stand and speak

With care – for if I can succeed with words,

Then things will come together happily.

Phaethon, your parents have begun to think

About your future and about this kingdom.

On you the weight will lie. You must begin

To share the precious burden. I grow old;

Even a king must sleep. Another hand

Is needed sometimes on the steering-oar.

You understand my meaning: the ship of state

Is safer with two anchors – even three.

One governor, one mind, may slip and fall –

Another in support is no bad thing.

So lend us your young strength, and double it

By marriage, for we know that marriage makes

A boy and girl into a man and woman.

Another man beside me on the throne
Will give the people confidence – and peace.

A new king growing up beside the old one
Shows there is freshness in the ancient stock,
And not a growing weakness as time passes.
Son, if we rule together we can stiffen
An old man's knowledge and wise hesitation
With youthful energy and fertility –
And keep the land in so much greater safety.
It would be strange if having won the throne
Through care and effort, we should lose it now,
And our just state become an anarchy.

If I should fall and you were not prepared,
Without a crown, without a place of power,
Someone would quickly steal your place from you –
A royal family has such enemies –
And you would mourn a father and a throne.
I was afraid something like that would happen –
But now you'll hold it safe from accidents
When I am dead; and when your mother dies
And you live on alone, you will stand firm
Because you're going to marry a good wife,
And not an ordinary mortal girl
But like your mother related to the gods,
A field for husbandry that any king
Would gladly tend, that all would envy him.

Meanwhile: the sun would watch and guard you overhead:
Under his holy eye you would be safe.

PHAETHON: Father, a boy that's offered half a throne –
Or even a footstool by the side of it –

Becomes a man as he breathes in the words.
This is an honour that I thank you for,
Now it is given. For it seems your judgement
That I am old enough and strong enough
To bear the weight and tame my wilder wishes
Under the yoke of time and circumstance.

But Father – I ask you to forgive my fears.
I am not so good or ready as you think.
To be a king – or even half a king –
Is hard: it's work; a sudden end to childhood.
I do not easily give orders, even
To servants. My sisters know, without a word,
All that I want, and keep me well content –
Without a word. I've lived a floating life,
Drifting from joy to joy, and now you say
It's time – today – to share the hidden work
That lies behind these luxuries and this pleasure.
I am not lazy – you know that – but, Father,
Give me more time, some training, time to think:
Then I would make a better king – like you.
But no, I see you think I will learn best
If suddenly thrown in. But to make me marry
Right at this time, another end to childhood,
Another change to all my settled ways –
Before I'm even thinking of a wife –
I fear the consequences. I'm too young –
I've never thought for anyone but myself.

CHORUS: The boy is sensible, my lord. These plans
Seem to have come a little suddenly.

MEROPS: Phaethon, we have talked about all this.
It seemed to me I'd proved the way to learn
Is to begin at once. And I shall be beside you
To counter your mistakes – if you should make them.

PHAETHON: You cannot be beside me in my bed,
Father.

MEROPS: Get in the chariot, son; and drive.

PHAETHON: No, listen, Father. I must speak of this.
You know the saying: a free man – like me –
With all the rights of any citizen,
Becomes a slave to serve the marriage bed,
His body being bought by what the bride
Brings in the marriage contract to his family.
This bride's a princess, very rich, immortal –
Child of the sun-god, constantly attended.
I'd know him watching from the sky each day
How I was treating her. How easily
My lightest fault could be avenged for her,
My briefest hesitation to obey
Be answered with the scorching of my country.
The daughter of Helios will expect much more
Than I can give her now. Let me wait, Father.

MEROPS: My plans have been conveyed to Helios now –
It is too late to change them. He'll have chosen
Which daughter he will give you as a bride.
She will have thought for days about the marriage
If you have not. Take a deep breath, my boy,
And dive. You do not have the choice. It is
Decided – whether you decide or not.

PHAETHON: A man must make his choices for himself.
　　When I get in the chariot, with the reins
　　Smooth in my hands, it is for me to choose
　　Whether I pull the right ones or the left,
　　Whether I turn my horses to the east,
　　To Helios' house, or to the world of Greece
　　And Italy beyond, the world you know
　　But I have never seen – and want to see
　　Before I settle in a stranger's arms.
　　I understand there are cities over there –
　　Towards the sunset – where the citizens
　　Govern the city and the state themselves.
　　They have no king at all, not one, not two.
　　How do they do it? I wonder is it right
　　For a whole country to be ruled by one,
　　Or even two, wise men who make the laws.
　　How can one man be wise enough for that?
　　You see, I have been thinking for myself.

MEROPS: How can a son of mine grow up so foolish?
　　The applauding crowd has clapped your wits away.
　　Indeed it is a folly of mankind,
　　In my view, to hand on the family goods
　　To children who have got no common sense –
　　Or power to the people in the street.
　　This cannot be: think what you're going to do:
　　Where would you go? Where would you find your food?

PHAETHON: Anywhere, Father; everywhere:
　　The nourishing earth will be my fatherland.
　　I might compete in the horse-race at Olympia…

MEROPS: Sit down, son. Calm yourself. I understand
    Your feelings, but you know a royal person
    Is not so free to act as you are saying.
    On the other hand, a clever person always
    Makes his own freedom. You will soon see how…
    But at this moment, true, you have no choice.
    It would be most unwise to anger Helios
    By the suggestion that you hesitate
    To marry one of his delightful children.
    You must be charming, a fine son-in-law
    That he might boast of to the other gods.
    And you can do it. I am proud of you.

PHAETHON: I am ready, father, if you think I am.
    I feel the greater strength for your opinion,
    Which gives me confidence to approach great Helios
    The terrifying god of heat and light,
    To ask for the divinely delicate hand
    Of one of his daughters. Then I can foresee
    With her beside me – and beside your throne –
    I shall be stronger still, no more a boy.
    For I have seen, even a full-grown man
    Grows when he marries, feeling in himself
    Greater solidity – he is less a ghost
    Than when he was an idle playful boy.
    I think that learning how to speak for two
    Gives him a greater curve of destiny,
    A longer life, and courage to continue.
    I feel all this already. Your good opinion
    Gives me the courage to accept a share
    In the kingdom – a stool beside the throne –
    And to proceed today to ask our neighbour

If I may take a daughter from his house
To be my wife. Give me your blessing, Father.

MEROPS embraces PHAETHON and goes into the palace. Exit HERALD also.

PHAETHON now speaks to himself.

PHAETHON: My mother says he does not know about me.
  Strange – but apparently it's natural –
  For rich men to be stupid. What's the reason?
  Can it be that because the god of wealth
  Is blind, the rich are blind as well? – and see
  Not even the simple truth of their own lives?

  But I have better things to think about –
  More urgent too. What am I going to do?
  What shall I ask great Helios when we meet
  For the first time? – not for a drink of nectar,
  Something much grander that will test his promise –
  Much more than generous hospitality
  Would give me anyway – something he'd grant
  Almost against his will, a special favour,
  A favour worthy of a god – and also
  Worthy of me, the new-arriving bridegroom…
  This is a test of who I really am,
  And it's a chance I may not have again.

Enter TUTOR.

TUTOR: The Queen has asked me to accompany you
  To Helios' palace. You might need some help,
  Or you might wish to send a message home.

PHAETHON: My mother does see clearly, and her plans
  Are better laid than mine. Come, my old friend,

Who taught me like a father, answering
My questions ever since I was a boy…

TUTOR: Is there a question troubling you now?

PHAETHON: I think I have to make my own decision,
But I am glad to have you coming with me.
I should not go alone to meet my bride,
Some grandeur is expected of a suitor.

I'll take my father's chariot…
He won't mind.
He can't object… This is my wedding day.

They go out toward the stables to arrange the horses and chariot.

CHORUS:
The days go silently; the years
pass in a rush.
The baby quiet in your arms
kicks on your lap,
stands laughing by your knees…
Now he can walk. Now he can walk away.

The boy entirely loved has gone
into the world.
He has found somebody unknown
outside to love.
He has found other arms.
He has turned away, and he will not turn back.

Today he enters a new life –
his childhood dies.
From now his body will belong
to his new bride
and never more to us.

This is why mothers weep on wedding days.
This is why mothers weep on wedding days.

Enter CLYMENE with NURSE.

CLYMENE: (*To CHORUS:*) Astonishing! We are ready to receive
    Our high-born guests. The palace is so clean –
    Even the oldest rooms, the furthest corridors –
    As if the gods had built it yesterday.
    You and your fellow servants have worked hard,
    To honour us, to honour the new bride,
    Who will be pleased: although this house is smaller
    Than where she was brought up, it may be cleaner.
    At least, we do not share a roof with horses.

    (*To the NURSE:*) This won't be easy, with the bride and
      groom
    Tongue-tied perhaps, and Merops feeling mortal
    Among so many gods – and the girl's mother –
    What is her name? I know she will be dazzling,
    A beauty comforted by lovely clothes…
    He could not give me anything so fine –
    A gift from him would have betrayed the child
    He gave me, the one gift I had from him,
    The greatest gift, dear Phaethon, whom I give
    Today to his new bride. What is her name?
    I have so little say in this… Like Phaethon,
    Who was disposed for kingship and for marriage
    By his impatient father – I mean, my husband.
    He tells me what to do and I must do it.
    Sometimes my secret is a kind of weakness,
    Impeding thought and action. I have more right
    To choose for Phaethon than my husband has,
    But I am forced to silence. Other times

My secret gives sweet comfort, and a joy
That no-one shares, the essence of my life.
But now there is a danger; Merops seeing
Helios and me together may suspect
Our friendly talk is too familiar,
Too easily intimate. Or Helios' wife
May see and suffer, and say something wild.
Even it might be Phaethon to speak
Openly, thinking there's no harm in truth.
It might be best to share the secret now,
Catch Merops in his happiness and tell him
Before the wedding feast – which will wash over
His angry moment and the possible danger.
No, it might spoil the day. You see, your mistress,
Even the daughter of Oceanus,
God of the water that surrounds the world,
Even the Queen of Ethiopia,
Where the gods come to feast when they are sad,
Has worries, secrets that disturb the heart
And make her hesitant and indecisive.
We worry about our children – specially
Our first-born – who remains our perfect child,
The definition of a son.
Dear friend,
Advise me – you can see I need advice
And you have given me good advice before,
Since our first days here, fresh from father's house,
New to the land of Merops. I shan't forget
You nursed me through the pain of Phaethon's birth –
When I called out on Helios you were by me
To muffle my despair, soothe my shocked mind

With homely words, persuade my tongue to silence.
Help me again with sensible advice.

NURSE: My Queen, what I advise could only be
    What you have thought yourself and often wished –
    That you had told him at some happy moment
    When Phaethon was younger. It is easy
    To wish for a solution in the past,
    But now it seems that fate may turn and tell him
    Not in your words, not in your gentle voice,
    But harshly, in the public view, the facts.
    Madam, you have had years to find a plan
    And have not found one. I have only had
    Today, since you told Phaethon the truth.
    How could I think of something new so quickly?
    But – I think Merops will be shamed and angry.
    It would be best if you could tell him first
    Before some rumour tells him what he is.

Enter MEROPS from palace.

Why, here he comes. Fate's giving you a chance
    To save yourself from dangerous revelations
    At this auspicious time. Tell him yourself
    Before perhaps some casual word from Phaethon
    Unsettles all that Merops has arranged.
    Shall I go in? Someone should see your daughters
    Are nicely dressed and ready for the feast.

Exit NURSE into the palace.

MEROPS: I am so happy. I had an old man's fear
    Of dying with my work half done, with no-one
    To finish it for me. Forgive me, dear,
    I came to bring you in out of the sun.

It does no good to wait out here for him.
He will not come till evening. That's the custom,
And I suppose the gods will follow it,
Perhaps with some amusement, in the dark,
With blazing torches, cries and showers of sweets.

CLYMENE: Merops, I came out here to ease my mind
Of little household thoughts and to regain
Control of my strong feelings. It is time
To tell you something that has troubled me
For many days.

MEROPS: Troubles? Today? My Queen,
With this alliance our country shall be strong.
No-one will dare to shake us – we'll be safe.
There will be children – some day I'll be called
Merops the First of Ethiopia.
The only difficulty might be the bride.
Helios has seen my daughters, all of them,
But I have not seen his. They will be lovely
Like ours, no doubt, but may be also proud.
A young proud woman is a fearsome thing
To share a house with. Even in a palace
One might sit trembling in another wing,
Sensing her anger. But I trust we'll live
With her as easily and happily
As we do now together.

CLYMENE: Merops, please
Listen and let me speak. It's true we live
Together easily – and happily,
But there is something that I have to tell you.

It is about our children... I mean, my son.
I want to tell you why I called him Phaethon.

MEROPS: Yes, yes, 'The Shining One' – That suits him now –
Very appropriate to his marrying one
Of Helios' daughters... Clymene! My dear!
Don't tell me you foresaw this marriage then
And named him so, to help him please the god!

CLYMENE: No, Merops, that was not what I intended
To say. I...

Palace door opens, enter SERVANT, hurrying. CLYMENE pauses.

SERVANT: O King, your daughters have prepared their song
To welcome home their brother and his bride.
They wish you would come in and hear it. You
Could better judge than they if they've done well.

MEROPS: My Queen, we may talk later, but the song
Must be made now as good as we can make it.

CLYMENE: Of course, you must go in. We may talk later...

To herself, as MEROPS goes into the palace.

Later, my King, may be too late for us.

CHORUS: O Queen, we guess you mean to tell
The King some fault. We think
That we can guess the fault. We think
It is important to confess
Before we are accused. The virtue
Of showing that we know our fault
Is cancelled when we're forced to show it.
Stained honour might be cleaned, renewed
In private, and the family

Keep the secret in private darkness,
Protecting both its name and ours;
But if the fault is known to all,
Who can support us? It is right
To tell your family what has happened
And let them judge it calmly.
You have done nothing wrong – except
Conceal a wrong that was done to you.

CLYMENE: Think of the women the gods have ruined
With false love – could I name them all,
There are so many? – Leda, Io,
Poor Lamia, lovely Antiope,
Semele dazzled, burnt to death –
Europa, Danae, Daphne, me…

CHORUS: Alcmene, Niobe, Callisto –
And we might name the boys as well,
Tithonus, Ganymede, Orion,
Adonis, Endymion, Anchises, Hymen
Whom Aphrodite raised to heaven
To be the god of weddings – and more
We shall never know, with their secrets hidden,
Their lives spoiled by the satisfaction
Of a god's burst of desire. I wish
We could clean such faults away in the river
Where we rub the dirt from our clothes and skin –
How much misery would be saved!

CLYMENE: But it's not a fault – it's not my fault –
It's Helios' fault! Helios the spy
The lovely watcher from above
Looked at me daily as I grew.

For I am a daughter of Oceanus –
I swam before I walked.
Swimming was never dangerous
For me, till Helios made it so.
He saw my body open in water
Like a morning flower stretching itself
And had to take me. Since then my life
Has been the hard life of the land…
Sea was my element and Helios
Should have kept out of it, let me be.
Cannot a god restrain himself?

CHORUS: O Queen, we are your lowest servants.
But we share the fortunes of your house.
What is good for you is good for us.
What threatens you endangers us.
If there is anything we should do
Tell us now and we shall do it.

CLYMENE: All I ask of you now is silence
About my secret, Phaethon's secret.
Keep the secret to yourselves.
I shall find my moment soon, today.

CHORUS: (*Solemnly.*)
You know how stories tempt us. So much pleasure
Passes between the teller and the listener.
But this one's yours, and we must leave it for you –
We shall restrain ourselves, unlike the gods.
We promise.

CLYMENE: That's all I ask for now. A solemn promise.
Even those gods must keep their promises…

I shall go rest, and try to wait with patience
Till Phaethon comes back and shows his bride.

Exit into the palace.

CHORUS: (*Sing.*)

Beauty is dangerous, like gold.
Everyone wants to hold it.
Everyone wants to own it.
They think of beauty as a precious stone.
It's more like a disease you must endure
With everybody offering a cure.

Eros is good with words – he says
Beauty gives all the pleasure.
This is not true – a fruit
Gives pleasure in its flesh not in its beauty.
He wants us to choose lovers by their rind,
Not by the juice, the taste, the tongue, the mind.

Men imitate the gods in that.
Good looks are all that matters –
Men want the rarer roses –
Not common flowers that everybody knows.
And so, the plainer blossom by the path
Escapes divine desire and human wrath.

Enter CLYMENE from palace, having changed her dress to be more splendid.

CLYMENE: A mother worries so about her son.
Is he behaving well, making a good impression?
He might offend his father Helios
By some quite unintentional word, some mortal
Vulgarity, a smell of sweat, some dirt.

I am so proud of him, I want his father
At this first meeting to see him at his best,
Looking like what he is, the child of gods
And worthy to be married to a goddess.
If Zeus can marry with his sister Hera,
Then Phaethon can marry one of Helios' girls.

Do I see dust? Is that the cheerful noise
Of horses in the courtyard by the stables?
Ah, there's my messenger, Phaethon's old tutor,
Come back to tell me all I want to know.

So how were you received by Helios?
I cannot tell by looking at your face.

TUTOR: Madam, I wish I could avoid that question,
And answer nothing. The bringer of bad news
Seems bad himself. I believe your son is dead.

CLYMENE: Phaethon is dead! What do you mean, you believe
My son is dead? Were you not there? What happened?

TUTOR: I can explain, but let me tell you slowly.
The terrible conclusion chokes and shakes
My voice, but we began so happily.

Madam, I went with him to Helios' palace
As you commanded. He accepted me
Without demur – he wanted company.
He took the royal chariot, the new one,
And the best horses, which I helped him harness.
We drove there rather slower than his usual –
Sedately, almost. He said nothing to me,
And I supposed he needed time to think.

Helios' palace is a sight to see:
I will say only we drove in through gates
With six of those heavenly diagrams on the left,
Six on the right – the stars the sun goes through.
I wanted to look longer; I imagine
The workmanship was...probably your cousin
Hephaestus made them?
Inside I stood far back –
The sun god's radiance – and I could not hear
Anything that they said, but I could see
Helios introduced your son to all his girls –
They named themselves and touched him, one by one –
All of them equally, it seemed to me,
As if the bride had not been chosen yet,
As if Helios wanted Phaethon to choose.
He seemed a little dazed by all their beauty,
The lovely similar faces of the sisters,
One of whom he should marry, all of them smiling
At ease among the glories of that hall.
Then Helios sat him down and made him drink
A little heavenly drink to steady him
And seemed to ask the purpose of this visit –
Of course he knew, but that is the polite
Observance between host and guest,
The girls sitting on cushions at their feet
Close to each other, smiling, their eyes shining
At the young man, who seemed to grow in size
Surrounded by such friendly admiration.
At last he stood – and seemed to ask his question,
Although he must have known by now the answer;
Helios had been so pleased and so attentive –
A glowing host, a parent very happy

To rise and to embrace his handsome son.
I could not hear the soft and almost modest
Admission of his fatherhood, but I saw it.

Then I could see your son was asking something.
Great Helios nodded, shining, like the sun
He drives across the sky – and then as if
A cloud had covered him, the glow was dimmed.
I thought some trouble had confused their talk,
Something had marred their mood. Had Phaethon
Been impolite? I could not think so –
His manner, even as a little child,
Was always courteous. A moment's silence,
And the young women in a group
Surrounded Phaethon – they were tall as him –
And took him by the hand and led him out
To the next hall where Helios had pointed.

I followed, thinking Phaethon had asked
For something Helios had not wished to give –
A precious object of the house perhaps –
But the girls laughing and affectionate
Taking your son by the arms were leading us
From hall to hall along to Helios' stables,
To see the heavenly horses with winged feet.
I thought as they walked down the line of stalls
Naming the radiant immortal creatures,
That Phaethon had asked for one. I thought
How would we feed it? It was worse than that.
The beautiful young women took bright harness
From golden hooks upon the stable wall
And yoked a team to Helios' chariot.

They did not seem afraid of those great horses
With feathery legs and puffing fiery breath.

I stood well back. Even your boy was daunted –
Not having driven four abreast before –
But seeing how the young girls danced around
The immortal chargers, calling them by name,
Seeing the immortal chargers taking care
To do no harm to bare feet and slim arms,
Phaethon, pale as moonlight, looked at me
As if he might have spoken. For a moment
I thought of saying, 'You could do it later',
But he went forward to the chariot step
And let his sisters kiss him.
He was reaching
To mount the glittering chariot when Helios
Called from the stable door: 'Rub on this ointment –
It will protect you from the rays of the sun –
My coursers know the way; but as you drive
Don't turn aside and enter Libyan air –
The desert dryness over Africa
Will use the axle as a fire-stick
And set the wheels on fire and wreck my chariot.
Hephaestus made it and I cannot ask him
To build another. So avoid the south:
Aim for the seven Pleiades instead.'
Phaethon bowed his head in acquiescence
Like a good son, then turned, grabbed at the reins,
Slapped them against the backs of his winged team
And set them off – they leapt into the lanes of air.
Helios rode behind, astride a horse
Named Sirius, shouting to his child:

'Drive that way, turn the chariot here, yes here.'
So they went up the steep part of the track,
The hooves and wheels making no noise in air,
So I could hear their words – directions, warnings –
Far in the distance.
The sun's too bright to look at,
But there's a pool beside the stable, full
Of some dull liquid that reflects the light.
There they can watch the chariot pass the signs
Of the zodiac and see where Helios rides
At any time, even so far away.
So we could keep our eyes on Phaethon,
As in a mirror, crossing the great sky.

The way is steep at first, the horses strain,
It must be easier to control their flight,
But where the track begins to level out
The horses started galloping. They went wild
Feeling the weakness of the driver's hands –
We saw in the great picture of the sky
They were no longer moving straight. The chariot
Began to leave a trail of smoke, that turned
From side to side. There was a flash of light
And something fell, leaving another trail
Down towards earth. We saw the chariot's track
Straightening out and going west as usual.
We knew that Helios must have boarded it;
We knew that Phaethon would not come back.
Helios' daughters all began to cry.
They had lost a brother and perhaps a husband.

They helped me find my way to where we'd left
Phaethon's favourite black chariot –

So ordinary now – and I drove back
To tell you what your brave son chose to do
With his one wish – and tell you how it ended.

CLYMENE: But where is Phaethon? I don't understand.

TUTOR: Phaethon must be dead. A bolt of lightning.
A fall from such a height. He must be dead.

CLYMENE: Where did he fall? Was it so far away?
Must I believe you? Is the dear child a corpse
Rotting unwashed up there in some ravine?
He might be still alive, and suffering.

TUTOR: I cannot tell. I only know
Your son was very brave – too brave.
I cannot think that he survived.

CLYMENE: How can I mourn, not knowing and not having
His body to lay out and bury here?
How do those women mourn their men who die
In battle and are buried far away,
Or never found to bury, never seen
Lying so still, eternally so still?
Phaethon, Phaethon, can you be dead?
Were you angry with us? Why did you do it?
Did you want to show your father Helios
You were his son, a charioteer?
O boastful boy, you have broken our hearts
With your bravery and your love of horses.
You were too young, you were always too young
For every wonderful thing you did.
It was always too soon, you could not wait
For greater strength, a full-grown body.
Hunting and riding you risked your life –

You thought I didn't know, but I knew:
The danger, the thrill, the rivalry of boys.

TUTOR: We only know your son
Tried something far beyond his powers,
And nobody – not even Helios –
Could have stopped him. I believe he's dead,
And we must start to think what we should do.

CHORUS: Young men are foolish in the face of danger.
Even their courage is a kind of folly.
A full grown man would have more sense
Than to try and drive such horses.

CLYMENE: To try – that was the danger. Boys will try
And not consider: what if it's too hard?
O Zeus, my son is dead. What shall I do?

CHORUS: Life seems unbearable now without him.
But you must learn to bear the pain.
You have other children, you have a husband –
You cannot turn away and grieve.
They must be told. They will grieve too,
And must be comforted.

CLYMENE: My husband, what am I going to tell him?
Can I spare him the pain? Can I keep it secret?
Who knows this happened? The gods will know,
But maybe we are the only mortals
Who know the story of Phaethon's fall…
No. Everyone knew where he was going –
To Helios' house, to fetch his bride.
O Phaethon, why did you have to drive
Today the horses of the sun?
On such a day – your wedding day.

(*To* TUTOR.) I shall go in. How am I going to tell them?

A man appears, coming from the country. CLYMENE *notices and turns back.*

CLYMENE: What do you want here? Who are you?

PEASANT: A farmer.

I come unwillingly, by the will of others.

I expect you heard, not long ago, a noise.

CLYMENE: No, but what sort of noise? I've been indoors.

PEASANT: Prepare yourself to hear your great misfortune.

CLYMENE: If you know something worth my hearing, say it.

PEASANT: I wish to speak to the ruler of this country.

I bring back to you the riches of your house.

CLYMENE: Tell me – I'll tell the King. We are as one.

PEASANT: The noise I heard was the crack of a thunderbolt

And from my field I saw its blazing track.

Something fell from the sky. Shall I tell all?…

It fell into the shadow of the earth…

I thought, This is important to the city,

And I felt sure I ought to tell the king.

May I not tell my story to King Merops?

CLYMENE: He shall be told, in time. Go on, speak frankly.

Out with the story – it may make you rich.

Pause. Offstage the princesses are heard performing their song, for MEROPS.

PEASANT: The whole city is mourning, full of grief,

But here… That music, that's a wedding song!

CLYMENE: Speak simply, as I advised you to before:
    And plainly – I was never good at riddles.
    Stop this confusion. Now. What is the matter?

PEASANT: My Queen, there is no sense in being angry
    With fate: there we are all confused and helpless.

CLYMENE: What do you mean? There is some sleight
     of tongue
    In this, some sense I do not understand.

PEASANT: We saw a body falling, not a star,
    A glorious sight even in that disaster.

CLYMENE: You said this…body…fell 'into the shadow';
    What sort of burial have you given it?
    Or is it hidden from us by its fall?

PEASANT: As I was coming through the town I heard
    A rumour: that today you had lost a treasure…

CLYMENE: And was there talk of finding it…this body?
    We want to know what happened, everything.
    It might be difficult. But we must try…

PEASANT: Madam, we have already found your son.
    We recognised him by his royal clothes.
    We did not wish to shock you with the sight.
    We thought his father should have seen him first,
    And told you the sad news a better way than this.

Body of PHAETHON brought on – his clothes still smoking.

CLYMENE: What is it? Phaethon! Phaethon! Who did this?
    Helios, was it you? Oh Zeus, my son is burnt to death.
    The vengeful goddess still plays about his body

And breathes up smoke and tongues of living fire.
I am done, I am weak as death; carry him in –

My husband! I can hear my husband near
Singing the wedding songs, leading the choir of girls.
Be quick, and wipe away the drops of blood,
If any of his blood fell on the ground.
Hurry then, hurry – for I want him hidden
In the stone chamber where the gold is kept,
My husband's gold – which I alone control,
Sealing the doorway with my signet ring.

O lovely beams of Helios, you have ruined me
As well as him. The name that mortals use
To call to you – Apollo – is the right one,
As if they knew its silent meaning: 'killer'.

*She goes in quickly with attendants carrying the corpse. Enter MEROPS
from side of palace with a choir of YOUNG GIRLS – PHAETHON's
sisters, dressed like bridesmaids – who sing this wedding song.*

YOUNG GIRLS: Hymen, Hymen,
    Bless this wedding.

    We praise the heavenly daughter,
    Daughter of Zeus.
    We praise you, lady Aphrodite,
    Queen of desires,
    Bringer of marriage to girls.

    We sing for you, loveliest goddess,
    Cyprian queen,
    For Hymen too, the one-day bridegroom
    You keep in heaven,
    Hidden child of your marriage.

We sing of your blessing with marriage
The King of our city –
Come from your golden starry palace
Where he is loved,
As he is loved by us.

Oh lucky Phaethon, king in fortune,
Who marry a goddess,
The only mortal to join in marriage
The immortal gods –
You will be famous.

Hymen, Hymen,*
Bless this wedding.

MEROPS: (*To one of his servants.*)
Run you, and take the girls indoors with you,
And tell my wife they are to dance in rings
And sing their hymns for all the gods at the altars
All round the house, their solemn wedding song,
And, specially, round the circular hearth of Hestia –
Where any wise man would begin his prayers:
Since Hestia is the first of all the gods
We name in prayers.
Afterwards they should leave the house and visit
The temple and make sacrifices there.

Exit SERVANT, who opens the door and immediately returns from the palace. Calls from the palace door.

SERVANT: Master, I had to turn and come back quickly.
The room where you keep all your treasured things
Of gold – through joins between the double doors

---

* *The myth about Hymen is that he died on his wedding day – like Phaethon.*

There's a black breath of smoke escaping. Peering in,
My face against the chink, I saw no flame
But the room inside is brimming with black smoke.
Come indoors now, for fear the god of fire
In a blaze of anger should burn down your hall –
At this most happy time of Phaethon's wedding.

MEROPS: What? See if it's not the smoke given off
By burning sacrifices drifting through the house.

SERVANT: I've looked at that – there's no smoke there at all.

MEROPS: Does my wife know? Has she not noticed this?

SERVANT: She's at the sacrifice – her mind is occupied.

MEROPS: Well, I'll go.
Such trivial things, if taken lightly, may
Bring down on us a great storm of destruction.
(*Prays*.) And may you, mistress of fire, daughter of
Demeter,
And you, Hephaestus, be kind and friendly to my house.

Exit MEROPS into palace.

CHORUS: How terrible I feel this! where oh where
Shall I set my foot now, either to fly
Off in the windy sky or to fade away
Into the underworld, invisible hiding place?
Wretched wretched this is!
Bad things are going to appear,
The unhappy queen and her son inside,
A corpse that has been hidden –
Awful to think of – and the fiery burning stroke
Of lightning thrown by Zeus –
And her affair with Helios.

46

Unhappy woman, immeasurable griefs:
Daughter of Oceanus, god of encircling sea,
Drop at your father's knees and pray his help,
To save your white throat from the slaughterer's knife.

MEROPS: (*Offstage.*) No. No. NO!

CHORUS: I hear the beginning of my master's grief.

MEROPS: (*Offstage.*) My child, my child! My son!

CHORUS: I hear him calling one who cannot hear.
    Now he can clearly see his poor son's fate.

MEROPS appears, to voice first a lyrical lament, then ordinary dialogue.

MEROPS: Oh gods! How could this happen?
    (*He yells with grief.*) Howl, howl!
    Go tell the singers of the wedding song to stop!
    Their lovely music is no longer fitting.
    The heavenly music rises
    But you lie low among the dead for ever,
    Burnt and disfigured now,
    No longer handsome for a bride.
    Your wedding songs are for Persephone,
    The wealth I would have left you, useless,
    Your cries unheard,
    Your torches not to light the wedding-feast
    But for the lonely dark.
    Dear you will be to us, as always;
    And anyone who pours an offering here
    Will say a prayer for you.

    Summon the tutor of my unlucky son –
    He went to Helios' palace with him. He

Knows both the good and bad that came of it.

CHORUS: Here comes the man, out of the palace, knowing
He must account for your boy's surprising death.

TUTOR has appeared, hesitating, at the palace doors.

MEROPS: Enough; come out of there; leave those doors alone
And explain to us – we're going to know the truth –
What happened to make my son die so, burnt up,
And miss the marriage we hoped for with a goddess.

TUTOR: Unlucky Phaethon, I must grieve for you.

MEROPS: You may groan later; now we need the story.

TUTOR: Phaethon, Phaethon, what a dreadful end.

MEROPS: You will cry twice as much if you don't answer.

TUTOR: Why do you make me speak of so much pain?

MEROPS: Who killed my son, and why? I must know that.

TUTOR: Master, I know, and yet I fear to say.

MEROPS: I may use force to get an answer from you.

TUTOR: Wait for a little till the grief subsides.

MEROPS: Better to know at once than live in doubt.

TUTOR: The one who killed your son can not be touched.

MEROPS: What do you mean? This is unbearable.

TUTOR: The father of gods and men destroyed your son
With a thunderbolt. That is the terrible fact.

MEROPS: This much I had begun to guess. Say more.
Why had the father of gods and men done this.

TUTOR: It was to save us all. For Phaethon
    Driving the chariot of the sun through heaven
    Had left the track – and would have burnt the world.

MEROPS: Phaethon went to visit Helios…
    Then did he steal the chariot of the sun?

TUTOR: No, my lord – Helios let him drive his chariot.

MEROPS: Helios let him drive his chariot. Why?
    The boy was much too young. I don't believe
    The god would let him risk his life like that.
    The child was going to marry Helios' daughter!

TUTOR: My lord, it happened. I was there. I saw
    Helios agree to let him drive the chariot.
    He was unwilling, but he let him try.

MEROPS: He was unwilling? Why should a god give in
    To the simple wish of any mortal man?

TUTOR: I cannot answer, for I could not hear
    How Phaethon argued to persuade the god.

MEROPS: Summon the Queen. Her father is a god.
    She may have better insight into this.

Exit TUTOR into palace.

CHORUS: The doings of the gods are strange to us.
    Sometimes it's better not to understand them.

    And in human life as well
    There are questions we should not ask,
    Boxes we should not open.

    Few of us have secrets
    Like Pasiphae, who loved a bull

And had a monstrous child,

But we all have something to hide,
Trivial faults and shames.
It is best to leave them alone.

MEROPS: I am the King. I shall ask what I want.
And my advice to you is to stay silent.

Enter CLYMENE from the palace.

MEROPS: Dear Clymene, we must bear this dreadful loss
Together, but I had to go outside
In the first madness of my grief. Forgive me
For running out and leaving you alone.
Your sadness must be even worse than mine.
He was the very centre of your life –
I understand that: you and he were joined
In some deep way that fathers do not know.

I have begun to talk and think again –
I thought that piercing pain would last forever –
But a new pain has started: of not knowing
How this could happen to our child. He was
Only a child – I saw that as I looked
At his small body lying on the cold
Stone floor among his half-burnt clothes, still smouldering.
How could this boy have got permission
To drive the immortal stallions of the sun?
Could I ask Helios? – but all day the god
Will be away driving the sun himself.

Your father is a god. You were brought up
Among divinities. Can you explain
Why Helios let a boy – even a boy

Who might have married one of his own daughters –
Try such a task, clearly beyond his strength?

CLYMENE: Merops, dear husband, I see why you must ask;
Kings must protect their people; you must know
How to protect us from our enemies,
How to avert disasters of all kinds.
You have a sense of danger we have not.
But, you remember our lost child was fond
Of horses, how he understood the beasts.
Isn't it natural, and like our son,
That when he was received by Helios kindly
He should have talked to him about his horses
And asked to ride – or drive them?

MEROPS: Clymene,
Gods are not fools. You know as well as I
Phaethon drove the chariot by himself –
He would have had to drive it all day long,
From sunrise here to sunset in the west –
As Helios himself is doing now. It's plain
Phaethon was not strong enough for that.
So why did Helios grant his stupid wish?
The gods refuse our prayers all the time.
Why give him what he wanted, and destroy him?
Helios must have known the consequence…
Why then would he agree? Had he no choice?
Clymene! Speak to me! Do you know the answer?
I think you do! The gods are sometimes bound
By fate as we are, by their promises,
By their own rules of hospitality…
Clymene, answer me! What do you know?

CLYMENE: Merops, dear husband – yes, I know why Helios
    Granted the foolish prayer of our dear son.
    It is a knowledge I have borne for years.
    I tried to tell you earlier, before...

    When you came courting to my father's house
    Beside the Ethiopian Sea,
    I was a lovely girl, and the all-seeing Sun
    Saw me one day while I was swimming, free
    In my last days of pure nubility,
    Warmed perhaps by your love and your attention.
    Helios fell in love with me. And what girl
    At that age has the strength to keep her chastity
    Safe from a god? The gods do what they want.
    And in his pleasure, smiling down at me,
    He promised me a favour I could claim
    When I had taken thought. My lord,
    Do not think ill of me – think of the others:
    Girls who say no to gods do not survive
    To tell their story to their families.

MEROPS: So Phaethon was not mine?

CLYMENE: You have not lost a son.

MEROPS: I had no son... And yet I loved the boy
    As if he were my son. The pain's no less.
    It is no consolation to discover
    My feelings were deceived. I loved the boy.
    The suffering is the same. But now – it appears
    I have lost you as well: my wife!
    You have been lying to me all these years.
    The small signs of affection, the caresses,
    Casual signals from a passing hand –

Were they lies too? Whose are my daughters?
Your early rising, every day – I noticed! –
You went to the window or the door
And looked up at the sky – you looked for him!
You meant to see him rise and pass, saluting
In mutual remembrance those embraces
Which you enjoyed in our first days of knowledge.
Clymene, is this our love? Was this our life?
A growing heap of lies? I was very near
To giving half my kingdom to a bastard!

CLYMENE: Merops, I understand your being angry –
But moderate your language about gods.
Consider also, why I lied to you.
Have you not had these many years of happiness
That you would otherwise have missed? A son
Who was a member of our family?
Who loved you as a father? who could not
Believe my story that he was not yours?
He went to Helios' house to ask the truth.
He must have asked the favour I was granted
So many years ago. He must have asked
To drive the chariot, and the god could not
Unswear the oath: he swore on the black river,
The Styx, that even the gods can not be false to,
That he would give me anything I asked for.
Merops, your love has given me everything
That I could want. Our marriage has been happy.
I never had to ask Helios to make good
His promise. I have never seen him since,
Since we… No, Merops, I have given you children,

Beautiful daughters born to both of us,
And everything a mortal man should want.

MEROPS: Except a true son. And a truthful life.
You have turned my life into a kind of story
For fools to laugh at. I'm the silly husband
Cuckolded by the god we all see daily.

As we stand here, I feel my memories rotting,
The good things going bad as Helios shines
On the body of my life where it lies dead
Behind me somewhere, as my son lies dead
Inside our palace where he used to live.
I recognise the rape was not your fault –
It was a sort of rape – against your will –
But then you lied. You filled the years with lies,
You even tried to hide the final truth,
Hiding his body in the treasury –
What were you going to do? To bury him
Alone, without my knowledge, so I'd think
He simply ran away from us and marriage –
Clymene, why? Why did you hide his body?

CLYMENE: I hardly thought at all. I only knew
You and the little girls – his sisters, Merops –
Were coming and would see that dreadful thing
Lying in horror at our palace door,
Cast like an accusation, black and burnt –
I had to spare them that.

MEROPS: O Clymene,
Your sympathy is tainted – I believe
You hid him in the hope of more concealment,
To save yourself, another kind of lie

Poisoning the trust of man and wife between us.
Even those years of love that stored my mind
With honey-like contentment have congealed
Like blood in painful crystals, and begun to crumble.
The stench of infidelity's in my nose
And will not leave me till I die of it.

If it were Zeus, then I might be avenged
By Hera; now, I must avenge myself
Or live forever in this daze of shame.

CHORUS: Oh gods, if ever you have loved mankind
    Or taken pleasure in us, save us now.

Lightning. Thunder. OCEANUS appears ex machina.

CLYMENE: Father!

MEROPS: Oceanus! Come to interfere…
    The family… The Olympian family!

OCEANUS: Merops! No need for anger – or alarm.
    You are my favourite of all the men
    My many daughters found. I have not come
    Around the world, across dry land, to harm you.

MEROPS: But you did harm me then, father Oceanus –
    Another kind of harm – but it was harm
    When you concealed from me that Clymene
    Had been before me tasted by a god.
    That is the cheap deception I was fed
    By your hospitable and her loving hands.
    When a man marries he must trust the family
    He joins his blood to – and my trust was given
    To you as well as to your dazzling daughter.
    The day I took her hand she was already

Bearing the seed of Helios in her body.
I was deceived, and you can hardly say
You did not know, for gods know everything.

OCEANUS: Merops – one moment. You speak out of turn.
What the gods know is not for you to judge.
What they ignore is not for you to know.
My daughter's secret was for her to tell you
In her own time, like any mortal woman.

MEROPS: She never told me Phaethon was not mine.
I found that out myself – the painful truth
Laboriously found. She let me love
That child, of whom I boasted to the world.
I was so proud of him, so pleased to see
His growing strength, his frank and honest mind,
His looks, his fatal courage... Phaethon!
Can you not bring him back to us, Oceanus?
I could forgive your daughter all, for that.

OCEANUS: Life is not given twice. The boy is gone
Where nobody can go to fetch him home
At evening. The river he has crossed
Is wider than the widest of my seas.
Merops, the boy was yours in every way
Except the tiny seed. Forget that seed.
What you must keep in mind is that your wife
Is not the guilty person. She was taken:
She did not do it – it was done to her.
Nobody can resist an amorous god.
The amorous god himself could not resist
The stir of beauty... If there was a fault
It was the fault of Eros, god of love.

It would be wrong to blame your wife for this.
She kept her secret through your happy time
Not for her own sake but to save you pain.
Clearly you cannot turn your sword on Helios;
That is unthinkable – but you must not touch
Your wife in anger. I can understand
The baffled impulse; but control your grief
And jealousy – do not throw your lives away.

MEROPS: You understand? You say you understand?
How can the gods have sympathy with us?
They never share our suffering. Clymene
And I must suffer now while you feel nothing.

OCEANUS: Again I tell you that you must not guess
What the gods know, what the gods feel or think.
Do you imagine you can understand
What Helios might be feeling now: he drives
The chariot on – and that is all you know.
Yet he has lost as much as you have lost.

Embrace my daughter, who has given you
So much, so lovingly and willingly,
And in her lonely wisdom hid the truth.

MEROPS: You find a mortal is so light and easy
He can forgive such wrongs.

OCEANUS: Embrace my daughter.
You are a king: you know there is a time
For Truth to hide, in shelter from the storm
Until the storm's forgotten. So it was
With Clymene: the shock and blaze of Helios
Had to become the secret of her life.

57

CLYMENE: O Phaethon, if only I had kept
    My secret in my heart, you would have lived.
    What Merops calls a lie had given you life;
    Telling the truth has only brought you death.

OCEANUS: Clymene, you had a duty to the boy:
    You had to tell him who his father was.
    Merops, you loved him too. You saw the best
    Of his short life, his beauty and his courage.
    It must not matter to you that he came
    As a god's gift: he was a lovely child,
    And loved you as his father all those years.
    His sisters weep for him: you must go in
    And comfort them.
    And think about a tomb:
    Let trees of this hot land drop perfumed tears
    And stretch their cool refreshing arms above him,
    And pilgrims come to visit at his shrine
    Here at the edge of the inhabited world.
    He is the honoured one, the bravest boy
    In the long history of the human race.
    Remember him with pride as well as tears.

He fades away.

CLYMENE: O Phaethon! Whenever I look up
    And see the sun, as long as I endure,
    I shall remember how you fell today –
    Alone and terrified and burned to death.
    Many will tell me that you chose, yourself,
    To drive the chariot that belongs to Helios.
    But it's not right for one so young to die.

The young should live, and wait their turn to die.
He had no chance to weep for anyone…

MEROPS: Give me your arm. Now I must turn my anger
To simple grief, try to forget the gods
Who meddle with our lives so wantonly;
And heal our pain in company with our daughters.
Then we may bury his uncorrupted body,
Purified by the lightning bolt of Zeus.

CLYMENE: I shall hang his belongings in the shrine:
I couldn't bear to see his bow again,
The curve of cornel wood, his little shield…
Goodbye to all the sports of childhood, o my dear…

Exeunt together.

CHORUS: The story of Phaethon will be told
In many ways:
As an example to the young,
A warning to the brave and bold,
His story will be played and sung
Until humanity's last days.

Appendix

The classical reader might well want to know in detail which bits of my version of Phaethon depend on a bit of Greek and which are 'translations of thin air'. Well, the answer to this is not easy: to start with, there are a number of lines here and there which were quoted by ancient writers and have been inserted in gaps where it was possible to do so. For these I refer the reader to James Diggle's edition of the play (Cambridge University Press, 1970, reprinted 2005) where it is easy to pick out these isolated lines or small groups of lines. Only one of these has any significance for the plot – Clymene's cry that her son's body might be 'rotting in some ravine' shows that she knows he is dead but that his body has yet to be found.

Then, the two surviving leaves of the full text are incomplete: they had been re-used to fill a gap in a smaller book; that is, they were cut down in such a way that each leaf starts with a column of text that has lost all but the last word or so of each line. This is followed (same page) by a column of full lines but the page has been cropped at the foot too, so lines are missing there. On the other side of each leaf there are again two columns of text, but of course this time the left-hand column consists of full lines and the right-hand column has only the first word or so of each line. In these circumstances I did my best to make my dialogue match the line-ends or line-beginnings but I cannot exactly tell where the invention ends and the translation begins. However, I may say roughly that the first leaf begins at Phaethon's line 'Father is sending me' (page 14) and ends at the end of Merops' first long speech ('Under his holy eye you would be safe', page 20); and the second leaf begins with the start of the puzzling dialogue between the peasant and Clymene (page 42) and ends in the dialogue between Merops and the Tutor, at the line 'The one who killed your son can not be touched' (page 48).

I mentioned in my initial note that I rewrote the scene with the deus ex machina. At first I thought that Aphrodite would be the right goddess to settle the dispute between Merops and Clymene, but later began to feel that Clymene might hope her father would come and save her. I myself think this is more likely to have been Euripides' solution, but producers of the play might like the option of using the ending with Aphrodite, which we print below.

*

CHORUS: Oh gods, if ever you have loved mankind
    Or taken pleasure in us, save us now.

APHRODITE appears, blazing, from some machine.

APHRODITE: Merops, you have forgotten that your wife
    Is not the guilty person. She was taken:
    She did not do it – it was done to her.
    Nobody can resist an amorous god.
    She kept her secret through your happy time
    Not for her own sake but to save you pain.
    Clearly you cannot turn your sword on Helios;
    That is unthinkable – but you must not touch
    Your wife in anger. I can understand
    The baffled impulse; but control your grief
    And jealousy – do not throw your lives away.

MEROPS: You understand? You say you understand?
    How can the gods have sympathy with us?
    They never share our suffering. Clymene
    And I must suffer. We suffer for your pleasure.

APHRODITE: The best part of your lives I have been watching
    Your royal marriage. Yes, it's my entertainment
    To see the marriage secrets slowly rise
    Towards maturity. And it's my work
    To make the team-mates of the marriage bond

Content together as they pull the family
Towards a future only I shall see.

You, Merops, have concealed from Clymene
The many small adventures of a man
Bursting with seed that must be broadcast somehow.
We shall say nothing of these little loves –
Clymene may have known of them perhaps
And wisely kept her peace. There is a time
For Truth to hide, in shelter from the storm
Until the storm's forgotten. So it was
With her brief ecstasy and her long secret.

CLYMENE: O Phaethon, if only I had kept
    My secret in my heart, you would have lived.
    What Merops calls a lie had given you life;
    Telling the truth has only brought you death.

APHRODITE: Clymene, you had a duty to the boy:
    You had to tell him who his father was.
    Merops, you loved him too. You saw the best
    Of his short life, his beauty and his courage.
    It must not matter to you that he came
    As a god's gift: he was a lovely child,
    And loved you as his father all those years.
    His sisters weep for him: you must go in
    And comfort them.
                 And think about a tomb:
    Let trees of this hot land drop perfumed tears
    And stretch their cool refreshing arms above him,
    And pilgrims come to visit at his shrine
    Here at the edge of the inhabited world.
    He is the honoured one, the bravest boy

In the long history of the human race.
Remember him with pride as well as tears.

She fades away.

CLYMENE: O Phaethon! Whenever I look up
I shall remember how you fell today.

MEROPS: Give me your arm. Now I must turn my anger
To simple grief, try to forget the gods
Who meddle with our lives so wantonly;
And heal our pain in company with our daughters.
Then we may bury his uncorrupted body,
Purified by the lightning bolt of Zeus.

CLYMENE: I shall hang his belongings in the shrine:
I couldn't bear to see his bow again,
The curve of cornel wood, his little shield...
Goodbye to all the sports of childhood, o my dear...

Exeunt together.

CHORUS: The story of Phaethon will be told
In many ways:
As an example to the young,
A warning to the brave and bold,
His story will be played and sung
Until humanity's last days.

Filling in the Gaps

Euripides wrote about ninety plays. Of these a handful (nine) were used in ancient education and so have survived from antiquity because there were many copies of them, but we have also an odd volume of Euripides' collected plays with eight more (it was the *Helen-Iphigenia* volume). The remaining seventy or so survive only as fragments, if at all.

'Fragments' is a technical term here: in this context it means normally 'lines or even single words quoted by other authors in antiquity'. Such quotations don't give much idea of what a play is about, as you can see if you try to guess what *Hamlet* is about from the lines that happen to have stuck in your mind. If 'To be or not to be' and 'Neither a borrower nor a lender be' suggest anything beyond themselves, it is not the actual plot of *Hamlet*. 'Mobled' and 'bisson' suggest even less of the subject and treatment.

However, a much more useful 'fragment' of *Phaethon* has also survived as well as such quotations: two leaves from an actual copy of the text. These leaves each originally had two columns of writing on each side, 40-odd lines in each column, so about 330 lines altogether. But the leaves were trimmed off at the foot (losing a few lines) so they could be used to repair another book which had two leaves missing. Moreover the book to be repaired was not only shorter but narrower, so the leaves were trimmed again (vertically, along the left-hand edge) and lost most of the column on that side – only a word or so was left of each line. If you try this out with a piece of paper and scissors after putting two columns of scribble on each side of the paper, you will find that you end up with a column of line-ends and a column of full lines on the front of the paper and a full column followed by beginnings of lines on the back: to sum up, line-ends, two full columns of text, and line-beginnings on each leaf. (If you want them to be like the real thing these leaves should now measure 240 x 202 mm and be parchment, not paper.) The mediaeval book-repairer then did his best to scrub the Euripides lines off and someone wrote the words missing from the new text (part of one of St Paul's Epistles, as it happens) on top of the faint lines of the old play. When these palimpsest leaves were noticed, in the eighteenth century, scholars were just able to read the Euripides words, part of the play *Phaethon*. The complete text of the play would have taken up perhaps as much as another eight leaves. As it is, the quotations and these two trimmed-down leaves give us 327 lines, somewhat less than a quarter of the play – and many of the lines are chopped short, at one end or the other. Is this enough information for a plausible reconstruction of the missing parts of the play?

Well, we know Phaethon was the son of Helios and we know he tried to drive his father's sun-chariot across the sky and couldn't manage it, and died. Also we have a 'hypothesis' (the argument of a play) which is itself only a fragment of papyrus, but it tells us that in this play Phaethon is the child of Clymene: she is married to Merops king of Ethiopia, but the child was conceived when she was seduced by Helios, and Merops doesn't know the child is not his. This, together with some of the literary quotations, fits very well onto the start of one of the palimpsest leaves so that it's clear the first scene of the play, the 'Prologos' (the 'talk before' [before the Chorus comes on and sings]), will have Clymene and her son, who will be talking about his paternity and the promise Helios made to Clymene that he would grant her a wish. The palimpsest leaf also has the entry of the chorus, so we know what the Chorus consists of: the women who keep the palace clean and shining and sweet-smelling; it has their first choral ode too; and it has the beginning of the next scene: a herald announces Merops and Phaethon. This scene will be a public confrontation between 'father' and son, mostly missing, but we can reasonably assume (from material in the Prologos, and the line-beginnings) that it will be about Merops' desire to share the burden of rule with his 'son' and also about the marriage Merops has arranged for Phaethon, to take place today, it seems.

We have therefore, after reading to the end of palimpsest leaf 1, a fairly firm idea of
- the Prologos
- the first choral ode (complete text in this case) and
- the second scene.

Now, at this point, several leaves of text must be missing. There is a substantial gap to be filled before our second palimpsest leaf begins. This second leaf has, to begin with, a column of line-ends that seem to be line-by-line dialogue (stichomythia) between two people. The second column of this leaf (a column of full lines) has Clymene exclaiming in horror at the sight of Phaethon's dead body, which is still on fire. Presumably Clymene was one of the two people talking a moment before, and the other was the person who brought the dead body to the palace. Since she doesn't immediately burst into a lyrical song of grief we can assume she knew already that Phaethon was dead – indeed we have some lines of what can only be the messenger speech, about Phaethon's beginning his great drive in the sun's chariot (one of the 'literary quotations' – actually from Longinus' essay 'On Sublimity') which must have been delivered somewhere between the two palimpsest leaves, so probably she learnt then, from the messenger, what had happened to Phaethon. Another of the 'literary quotations' (from Plutarch this time) backs this up: she is quoted as saying something about 'the one who is dear to me, rotting unwashed in some ravine, a corpse', a remark that shows there is a point at which she knows he is dead but that the body has not been found.

So now we can begin to reconstruct what was in the gap:
- scene with messenger speech, followed by
- choral ode, presumably, and then by this new
- scene in which Phaethon's body is brought on stage.

This scene (still on side one of this second palimpsest leaf) continues with Clymene hearing her husband coming, accompanied she says by a choir singing the song composed for Phaethon's wedding. She has her servants pick up the body and take it into the palace, to hide it in a place where only Clymene has the key. (To *hide* it? What is she thinking of?) The text continues further: Merops comes onto the empty stage with a choir of young girls who sing the wedding song for Phaethon, a horrifying bit of dramatic irony. Merops sends the young girls off to sing elsewhere but almost immediately a servant comes from the palace to say there is a fire there. Merops goes to see to it and discovers that his 'son' is dead. He returns on stage and has the Tutor summoned, and begins questioning him ... and the text runs out.

It is surely clear that the remaining leaves of the play would have shown Merops gradually finding out why Phaethon had been allowed to drive Helios' chariot (Helios had no choice, because of his promise to Clymene) and that his son was not his son and that his dear wife has been lying to him for years. It seems permissible to deduce that there will be a marital row at this point, pacified finally by the appearance of a deus ex machina. It has been argued that other mythical Greek husbands – not to mention St Joseph – whose wives were impregnated by a deity were actually pleased by this 'honour' and that therefore there would not be a row. But Merops had been deceived by Clymene, a very different situation, and he had rejoiced in the son, publicly, for many years now, as his own. His view of his life has been profoundly shaken. At any rate, I feel sure we must have, as final episodes of the play,

- a scene between Clymene and Merops, probably tending towards violence, and
- a deus arriving ex machina, to bring the play to a peaceful conclusion.

This outline seems pretty well certain, but when I had filled it in by translating the fragments and inventing the rest ('translating thin air') – the missing choral odes and the missing dialogues and the scene with the messenger speech – what I had was still shorter than any of the rest of Euripides' complete plays. I didn't think my scenes and odes were too short: I had taken care (for instance) to make Phaethon's speeches to his father as long as Merops' speeches to Phaethon, as in other Euripides plays; and I didn't want to dilute them by expanding. I concluded that there must have been at least one other scene

– probably before the scene with the messenger's narrative. What did it contain?

*

Now the above account is rather simplified, and passes over several problems that had to be resolved immediately and some that might be allowed to wait. During the process of translating what had survived and filling in what had *probably* once been there, as described above, the translator's mind was of course continually aware that every piece of phrasing implies a context and what one may call a field of expectation, a glimpse of the rest of the landscape. It was necessary to keep some bits of the landscape blank – open if you prefer.

The most important of these options to keep open seemed to be the question of what the messenger had seen and the allied question of whether he told all he had seen to whoever he made his report to. It is clear that the report must have been made to Clymene alone, because Merops later on still doesn't know anything about what has happened in the sky. This has implications about the relationship between the messenger and Clymene – surely he would have been expected to report to Merops as well. (Later in the play, the person who brings the dead body on stage seems to want to speak to Merops rather than to Clymene alone, and this must have a different implication.) At any rate, I think we must accept James Diggle's argument that the messenger was the Tutor, who had accompanied Phaethon to Helios' palace and was reporting back. Unfortunately, here I took a wrong turning: I thought at this stage that Diggle was also suggesting that possibly the Tutor had not seen the whole accident; and therefore I should keep this possibility open, which caused me to write a first draft of the messenger scene with an inconclusive ending. Later I realised that Clymene knew of Phaethon's death before she had his body to bury, so I saw that she would have said her sad line (the one Plutarch quoted) just after the messenger had told her the *whole* story. (Very much later, in fact after I had finished writing, I saw that Diggle made this point himself.) I now concluded that the original messenger did see the catastrophe and does report it in his long narrative speech: that must be how Clymene knows Phaethon is dead even before the body is brought to her. Also, this reading of the plot reinforces the argument that the messenger is the boy's Tutor reporting directly to the queen, possibly because he knows her secret, the paternity of Phaethon, or perhaps because she has asked him to accompany Phaethon and to report back specifically to her.

Now what about the big question: why does Clymene try to hide Phaethon's dead body from Merops? Such an action must mean that Clymene is still hoping at least to delay, if not put off altogether, Merops' finding out not just that Phaethon is dead but why he is dead. Presented to us so abruptly in the fragment of palimpsest, immediately after the shock of seeing Phaethon's smoking body, her action is surprising, even baffling, but if it had been considered before, the audience would be shocked perhaps, but not completely taken aback. I conclude that Clymene has wondered (in a lost passage) whether she needs to tell Merops he is not Phaethon's father – the peaceful marriage might go on as before. She told Phaethon because he might soon become a father, so he ought to know the facts; but now he is dead, she might be able to forget the whole thing. Merops is old and might die none the wiser, thinking Phaethon had run away to see the world – or something. Might such considerations explain her trying to hide the corpse? It is presumably done on impulse, without enough thought. (Surely somebody is ultimately going to say something in front of Merops that reveals the truth.) To sum up, all this persuaded me that in the lost scene, among other things, Clymene had to think again about the danger of Merops' finding out about Phaethon's true paternity. If, for instance, in the lost scene she tells Merops the facts today, the wedding day, Merops is hardly going to cause a fuss, if no worse – and (from the playwright's point of view) she would appear in a better light.

Another problem was the matter of the Herald. Presumably on Merops' orders, the people are specially summoned, in this official and formal way, to hear about Phaethon's marriage – but then, instead of briefly announcing the wedding and dismissing his subjects, Merops begins what is evidently going to be a long speech; and it seems equally evident that Phaethon, also at length, is going to resist his supposed father's plans for him to marry and share the throne. Does this family argument really all get played out in public? We can't know, for the text is missing. After much agonizing I decided that would have to be a decision of the producer: Merops would simply wave the Herald away, perhaps, when he saw this was becoming embarrassing, and the Herald would quietly dismiss the imaginary audience of Merops' subjects. Or else Merops and the Herald would ride out the embarrassment, because after all Phaethon does seem to acquiesce in the end (as I have it).

There was one most difficult piece of surviving text, the incomplete dialogue at the beginning of the second palimpsest leaf, the thirty-six line-endings that precede the abrupt description by Clymene of Phaethon's burning body. It seems to me that the two speakers here, one of whom must be Clymene, are being deliberately mysterious to each other. (This is apart from their being mysterious to *us* because of the amount of text that is missing.) The second speaker is surely someone who has brought Phaethon's body to the palace. Now he is being mysterious, not explaining himself, and trying to insist on seeing the king, for several reasons: I imagine he is afraid to be the messenger of bad news; he wants a reward; he thinks that a child's body should be returned not just to his mother but to both parents, or perhaps to the father (after all, the king) if necessary; it is difficult to do what you think is right when confronted by an imperious queen, but he does want to do the right thing by the dead person and he feels some social slipperiness is the only way. She, for her part, is trying, without being too obvious, to make him cough up his information without bringing Merops into it; for she has a sense (as one does when the phone rings or as one used to when there was a knock on the door) of what the information will be about. So the lines contain a good deal of fencing in the dark, and we are probably never going to get the moves exactly right. However, it does seem that the queen keeps asking him to speak plainly ('free' – from fear, presumably, line 193) 'as I ordered you before' line 197) because she is not 'good at guessing' (line 198). A few lines later we have the words 'burial' and 'corpse' just before the missing six lines at the foot of the column. It seems clear to me that the scholars François Jouan and Herman Van Looy are mistaken, in their Budé text of the Euripides fragments, to insert here, at this point, Clymene's line about the corpse lying rotting in a ravine, just before the actual smouldering corpse is produced. I think I have shown above that the natural context for her line would be directly after she hears that her son is dead but before his body has been found (i.e., at least a scene earlier). Classical Greek narrations often separate these two moments, and it seems most likely this is the situation here. Further, her satisfaction at getting the body to bury helps to explain her *not* going off into an emotional outburst of lyrics here. (She must have done that already, earlier.) It seems to me that, however the jumble of end-words in these lines is forced into making a coherent exchange, their main outline is now clearer: the person bringing Phaethon's body wants to present it to both of the child's parents, from an obscure sense that this is proper, and Clymene has very likely guessed why he has come and is trying to keep the tragedy to herself.

There are three other problems to mention, gaps in the plot. Two are minor, but some scholars seem inclined to take them more seriously than an audience would. One is: who was Phaethon supposed to be going to marry? Since he dies before the wedding, does it matter? – one might say. The obvious candidate for his bride would seem to be one of Helios' daughters (certainly not Aphrodite, much too grand – and too old – for him). This would help explain the story that the Heliades, Phaethon's sisters by his father, wept so much that they were changed into trees: they had all lost a brother, but one of them (and maybe they didn't know which) had also lost a handsome husband. The other small problem is, who are the girls who sing the wedding song, on a stage only just cleared of Phaethon's burning body? Again, we don't know, but Diggle suggests they might be Phaethon's sisters by his mother, and this seems to me not only tidy but right.

Finally, it seems generally agreed that a god must appear at the end to resolve the serious dispute between Merops and

Clymene – but which god? James Diggle briefly names some possibilities, and I at first chose Aphrodite from his list, as a suitable deity to remedy the troubles she had herself caused. It was almost a joke that made me change my mind and rewrite the final scene for Oceanus. The idea was not so much that he was Clymene's father and would protect her, or the fact that at one point the Chorus recommends her to call to him for help; it was really the hope that perhaps the director of my version of *Medea*, Jonathan Kent (a devotee of water in the theatre), would be swayed by the chance to portray the god of water on stage. The idea was trivial, but acting on it produced a serious improvement, for I believe Oceanus makes a better resolver of the conflict than Aphrodite would.

*

It might seem to the reader that a translator would have done all the logical work on the plot of the play before beginning to reconstruct the text in detail. But I did not: I began writing the beginning as soon as I understood what the first scene would contain, leading up to the point where I would meet, and have to make sense of, the incomplete lines of the first leaf of text, and then translate in the usual manner the full lines of the rest of the scene, the first ode of the Chorus, and the beginning of the second scene. That would give me a firm basis for continuing with that second scene, between Phaethon and his supposed father Merops, and then perhaps even the scene with the messenger's speech.

The writing had been surprisingly easy – up to the first draft of the messenger speech; and it was only after that point that uncertainty about the plot made it difficult to continue. Of course every speech written had implications for the direction of the rest of the play, but then the main lines of the play were clear and one just had to keep within them. The situation was much like that of writing an original poem – except that in this case the boundaries of the work were less fuzzy, and could not be altered. Even expanding the damaged lines proved straightforward in some cases – the beginning of Merops' first speech runs pretty smoothly, I think, and doesn't betray its similarity to a Victorian parlour game ('bouts rimés'). So it was only after I had written those first scenes and translated the whole of the rest of the 'fragments', and added (along the same trajectory) an ending, that it was obvious my reconstruction was too short and the hard thinking about the plot began, as described above.

This hard thinking sometimes took place when I woke in the night (perhaps because of the unconscious delight of finding a solution to a problem), or at odd times of day. Sometimes the solution came in the form of some lines (to be jotted down) or as a topic that should be dealt with. (These fragments would usually stimulate the production of further lines when they were entered in the current draft.)

I had hoped the work would give me some idea how a fifth-century playwright chose for example the subject of an ode for the Chorus, but really I am no clearer about this than I was before: the subjects of odes presented themselves as poems always do present themselves, in a vague blur of purpose with perhaps some opening words, and they crystallised as the lines were written. When I translated *Medea* some years ago I thought perhaps the odes of that play might have been written *after* the whole work of the dialogue had been written, but though that may have been the procedure on occasion, I think now that sometimes at least the odes were written on the spot, as the playwright finished a scene of dialogue, the subject of the dialogue suggesting the subject of the choral ode. There is a story that Euripides' son sometimes helped with the choruses, and if this meant he sometimes worked on the words, that would explain the variable quality of the lyrics – I thought and still think that the famous first chorus of *Medea* is all but incoherent.

Archaeologists sometimes sharpen their understanding by attempting to reproduce an ancient object or solve a technical problem without using modern equipment. To some extent that sort of practical archaeology was what I was doing. I wish I could say more about this, but instead of gaining much insight into Euripides' mind and modus operandi, I merely came away with an even more intense admiration for a man who could write four excellent plays in twelve months, let alone perhaps produce and direct them himself – year after year.

*

I should add that I only read Goethe's attempt at a reconstruction of *Phaethon* much later, after the dust had settled and my version had been completed. It was then too that I learned from a chance conversation with Adrian Mitchell that Thomas Love Peacock was another man who tried to revive the play. Neither of these earlier attempts made me rethink anything I had written, interesting as they were.

Finally, I must again express my gratitude to Professor Diggle for information and offprints and for a number of comments he generously made on a translation of the 'mysterious lines' which I sent him. His edition of *Phaethon* (Cambridge University Press, 1970), which was all I used, is now available as a paperback. The Greek text (with an English translation *en face*) can also be found in *Selected Fragmentary Plays of Euripides*, vol. 1: *Telephus, Cretans, Stheneboea, Bellerophon, Cresphontes, Erechtheus, Phaethon, Wise Melanippe, Captive Melanippe*; edited by C Collard, M J Cropp and K H Lee (Aris and Phillips, 1995).

Alistair Elliot
Newcastle upon Tyne
November 2007